My Favourite Things

Name..

Address..

....

Date..

If you really want to understand what sort of person you are then you won't do better than to think about the books and films you like.

If you want to know the sort of person you would like to be then you would do well to think about those whom you love and admire.

If you want to remember good times in your past then it's nice to remember music that you have enjoyed and places you have visited.

If you just want a good supper then it's useful to be able to recall a really good recipe!

And, if you simply enjoy making lists, this book will give you hours of pleasure.

Enjoy!

My Favourite Films

Titles   Ratings

One of my favourite films

Title:

When I saw it:

Starring:

Synopsis:

My star rating:

One of my favourite films

Title:

When I saw it:

Starring:

Synopsis:

My star rating: ☆☆☆☆☆

One of my favourite films

Title:

When I saw it:

Starring:

Synopsis:

My star rating: ☆☆☆☆☆

One of my favourite films

Title:

When I saw it:

Starring:

Synopsis:

My star rating: ☆☆☆☆☆

One of my favourite films

Title:

When I saw it:

Starring:

Synopsis:

My star rating:

One of my favourite films

Title:

When I saw it:

Starring:

Synopsis:

My star rating: ☆☆☆☆☆

One of my favourite films

Title:

When I saw it:

Starring:

Synopsis:

My star rating:

One of my favourite films

Title:

When I saw it:

Starring:

Synopsis:

My star rating:

One of my favourite films

Title:

When I saw it:

Starring:

Synopsis:

My star rating:

My Favourite Books

Titles   Ratings

One of my favourite books

Title:

When I read it:

Main characters:

Synopsis:

My star rating:

One of my favourite books

Title:

When I read it:

Main characters:

Synopsis:

My star rating: ☆☆☆☆☆

One of my favourite books

Title:

When I read it:

Main characters:

Synopsis:

My star rating:

One of my favourite books

Title:

When I read it:

Main characters:

Synopsis:

My star rating: ☆☆☆☆☆

One of my favourite books

Title:

When I read it:

Main characters:

Synopsis:

My star rating: ☆☆☆☆☆

One of my favourite books

Title:

When I read it:

Main characters:

Synopsis:

My star rating: ☆☆☆☆☆

One of my favourite books

Title:

When I read it:

Main characters:

Synopsis:

My star rating:

One of my favourite books

Title:

When I read it:

Main characters:

Synopsis:

My star rating: ☆☆☆☆☆

One of my favourite books

Title:

When I read it:

Main characters:

Synopsis:

My star rating:

My Favourite Music

Titles   Ratings

One of my favourite pieces of music

Title:

When I first heard it:

Who wrote it or played it:

Why I like it:

My star rating:

One of my favourite pieces of music

Title:

When I first heard it:

Who wrote it or played it:

Why I like it:

My star rating: ☆☆☆☆☆

One of my favourite pieces of music

Title:

When I first heard it:

Who wrote it or played it:

Why I like it:

My star rating:

One of my favourite pieces of music

Title:

When I first heard it:

Who wrote it or played it:

Why I like it:

My star rating: ☆☆☆☆☆

One of my favourite pieces of music

Title:

When I first heard it:

Who wrote it or played it:

Why I like it:

My star rating: ☆☆☆☆☆

One of my favourite pieces of music

Title:

When I first heard it:

Who wrote it or played it:

Why I like it:

My star rating: ☆☆☆☆☆

One of my favourite pieces of music

Title:

When I first heard it:

Who wrote it or played it:

Why I like it:

My star rating:

One of my favourite pieces of music

Title:

When I first heard it:

Who wrote it or played it:

Why I like it:

My star rating: ☆☆☆☆☆

One of my favourite pieces of music

Title:

When I first heard it:

Who wrote it or played it:

Why I like it:

My star rating:

My Favourite Places

Where   Ratings

One of my favourite places

Where:

When I first went there:

Why I like it:

My star rating:

One of my favourite places

Where:

When I first went there:

Why I like it:

My star rating: ☆☆☆☆☆

One of my favourite places

Where:

When I first went there:

Why I like it:

My star rating:

One of my favourite places

Where:

When I first went there:

Why I like it:

My star rating: ☆☆☆☆☆

One of my favourite places

Where:

When I first went there:

Why I like it:

My star rating:

One of my favourite places

Where:

When I first went there:

Why I like it:

My star rating: ☆☆☆☆☆

One of my favourite places

Where:

When I first went there:

Why I like it:

My star rating:

One of my favourite places

Where:

When I first went there:

Why I like it:

My star rating: ☆☆☆☆☆

One of my favourite places

Where:

When I first went there:

Why I like it:

My star rating:

My Favourite People

Names Ratings

One of my favourite people

Name:

When I first met or heard of him/her:

Why I like, love and admire him or her:

My star rating:

One of my favourite people

Name:

When I first met or heard of him/her:

Why I like, love and admire him or her:

My star rating:

One of my favourite people

Name:

When I first met or heard of him/her:

Why I like, love and admire him or her:

My star rating:

One of my favourite people

Name:

When I first met or heard of him/her:

Why I like, love and admire him or her:

My star rating: ☆☆☆☆☆

One of my favourite people

Name:

When I first met or heard of him/her:

Why I like, love and admire him or her:

My star rating:

One of my favourite people

Name:

When I first met or heard of him/her:

Why I like, love and admire him or her:

My star rating: ☆☆☆☆☆

One of my favourite people

Name:

When I first met or heard of him/her:

Why I like, love and admire him or her:

My star rating:

One of my favourite people

Name:

When I first met or heard of him/her:

Why I like, love and admire him or her:

My star rating: ☆☆☆☆☆

One of my favourite people

Name:

When I first met or heard of him/her:

Why I like, love and admire him or her:

My star rating: ☆☆☆☆☆

My Very Favourite Recipes

What it is   Ratings

One of my very favourite recipes

What it is:

Ingredients:

Method:

My star rating: ☆☆☆☆☆

One of my very favourite recipes

What it is:

Ingredients:

Method:

My star rating: ☆☆☆☆☆

One of my very favourite recipes

What it is:

Ingredients:

Method:

My star rating:

One of my very favourite recipes

What it is:

Ingredients:

Method:

My star rating: ☆☆☆☆☆

One of my very favourite recipes

What it is:

Ingredients:

Method:

My star rating: ☆☆☆☆☆

One of my very favourite recipes

What it is:

Ingredients:

Method:

My star rating: ☆☆☆☆☆

One of my very favourite recipes

What it is:

Ingredients:

Method:

My star rating:

One of my very favourite recipes

What it is:

Ingredients:

Method:

My star rating:

More Favourite Things

What	Ratings

One more of my favourite things

My star rating:

One more of my favourite things

My star rating:

One more of my favourite things

My star rating:

One more of my favourite things

My star rating:

One more of my favourite things

My star rating:

One more of my favourite things

My star rating:

One more of my favourite things

My star rating:

One more of my favourite things

My star rating:

One more of my favourite things

My star rating: ☆☆☆☆☆

One more of my favourite things

My star rating:

Printed in Great Britain
by Amazon